A WALK TO ETERNAL
love

The Spirit's Destiny

CARLOS MEDINA

Copyright © 2019 by **Carlos Medina**

All rights reserved. No part of this publication may be reproduced, distributed or transmitted in any form or by any means, without prior written permission.

Carlos Medina / Magesoul Publishing
PO BOX 580019
Bronx, NY 10458
www.magesoul.com

Publisher's Note: This is a work of fiction. Names, characters, places, and incidents are a product of the author's imagination. Locales and public names are sometimes used for atmospheric purposes. Any resemblance to actual people, living or dead, or to businesses, companies, events, institutions, or locales is completely coincidental.

Edited by **Soshinie A. Singh**
Cover artwork from **Shutterstock**

Bulk purchases from Magesoul Publishing are available with discounts.

A Walk to Eternal Love / Carlos Medina -- 1st ed.
ISBN 978-0-9980403-3-2

DEDICATION

This is a reminder to the despondent souls that true love is out there, and the walk is very much worth it.

Do not lose hope. You will find your partner to walk eternally with, one day.

CONTENTS

	Dedication	i
1	Body	9
2	About the Author	129
3	Connect with the Author	130

Save your heart
For the one who is ready
To walk the eternal path
Of love with you.

You will know them
When you feel them

I want us to be that couple which grows old together. The one that has ups and downs. The one that finish each other's sentences. Yes. That couple. The one that cooks for the other. The one that does many things together. The one that you can't wait to get off work for because you missed being with them so much. The one you can share your life with. The one that you can trust and not worry about a thing. That kind of couple. The one that you don't have to hide yourself, and can just be you. The one that sits on their porch and just watches the sky while drinking coffee. The one that can sit in front of a fireplace and just admire the beauty the other holds. That couple that will love each other for eternity. That couple that communicates to each other about everything. That couple that can love each other with depth. A love that only comes from somewhere deep within. A couple that believes in unity.

If he loves you. He'll show it to you. There are many ways for a man to show his love. You just need to pay attention. It could be the smallest things. A gesture, a look, or a touch. You can feel it in the tone of his voice. The way he speaks in a relaxed way. Also in the way he speaks about you. The way he occasionally wears your favorite color. The way he respects you. Pay attention to those little details ladies. It will show you just how much he cares.

Sometimes, the person your soul desires is not the best looking one or the most famous one. Sometimes, it's the silent one. The shy one. The so called "weird one". Those are the ones that hold a lot of passion within. They know how to love every shattered piece of you.

You're the simple one inside, yet to others you're complicated. You love, and you know how to love hard. It might feel lonely and depressing. But you know that you just can't give your love to just anyone. Take it easy and have patience. Perhaps financially you're struggling, but you have been in worst situations. Don't fall for someone just for the need to have someone by your side. Wait for the right one. Not the one that will try to get in bed with you. But the one that is willing to be there with you. That one person that sees a future with you.

And if I could live the rest of my life, loving you, cherishing you and understanding you. To me that's a life well lived.

How couldn't I be passionate? When within every single heartbeat there is the echo of my love bursting through.

Learn to swim with me in the ocean of love.

There is nothing more beautiful than a person who has ambition, a caring heart and a soul full of light.

Just one glimpse into her eyes, and I saw the many colors of the rainbow.

A WALK TO ETERNAL LOVE

I want to make love to you under the moon, and hear our screams while your soul is deeply penetrated by my love for you.

It was her soft skin, that made me trace my lips over her. It was her gentle touch that made my thoughts undress her. Following her heartbeats allowed me to explore her entirely. But listening to her spirit calling me every full moon, was her way to scream, come make love to my soul.

We created a fairy tale with each one of her thoughts. It was our way of making dreams become reality.

It was her hidden love, dripping right into my heart, creating magic. Resurrecting my soul to reach out and touch her.

My heart rehearsed all the silent notes that came from my soul, hoping that late at night it will sing to you all your favorite lullabies.

My soul is like a wildfire ready to burn down all the walls around your heart.

And when our dreams unite, allow me to be your personal artist. I want to use your body as my canvas, creating beauty on top of beauty. Brushing my lips on all your curves, cherishing you from head to toe.

Master the art of touching her mind, and watch her soul make love to you.

Learn the way her mind works. Understand every need she has. It's not always about you. When you stimulate her, she will open up the gateway for you.

I may not be able to paint the rainbow over the sky for you, but I'll reprogram my soul for you. I'll erase the bad memories and stitch up my heart, just to be an echo of your love.

A WALK TO ETERNAL LOVE

All relationships will have their ups and downs. It's unavoidable. But two individuals with the same goals, offering each other stability and security - that no matter the obstacles, will be together in unity. That's a beautiful relationship. That's the kind of relationship I seek.

To understand my love, you must understand my depths and acknowledge your soul.

No words needed to be said, for it was written all over her.

Her eyes speak the language not many can understand, for they show the amount of pain she lived in her past.

She has the presence of a queen and the beauty of a goddess, but I know deep inside she has the most fragile heart. She seeks and seeks for that soul which can commit to her, the one that will trust her, care for her, build with her, that rare soul. That unknown soul.

When someone loves you, they accept you for who you are. They won't try to change you. They will take you in their arms without hesitation. They will protect you and be there with you.

Can I use my lips to write poetry all over your body? Just like the ones you read here. I promise it will be high definition.

Here. Take my halo, for my wings have already been surrendered to you.

Give me your heart, for tonight I shall hang it up on the walls of my soul to cherish and remember why I believe in this magical love.

Everything I ever wanted to say, is written all over your soul. Just close your eyes and listen to all those silent words.

Can I rest all my worries upon you? Can you promise to be there in the darkest times?

Even though these walls that you built are so tall. I will keep climbing. I won't stop. I won't look back. It's my only chance to get to your side. It's my way of showing you, I'm built different from the rest.

Together we'll set the clock in to motion. No looking back. We will be two souls, moving in the same direction, second after second, minute after minute, hour after hour, till eternity.

All relationships begin like a page from a fairytale. The beginning is probably the best part. Love is in the air. The romance is at its highest. Yes. That stage of getting to know each other. The one where you both speak to each other for hours. That stage that you just can't get enough of the other. You begin wanting to know every single thing in that person's life. From the time they wake up, to what time they go to sleep. You just want to make sure that person is thinking about you throughout the entire day. It's a beautiful stage, isn't it?

What happens afterwards? You come to a point where the priorities change. It's no more my love and babe. You don't feel the same way about that person. You love them. But in the back of your mind you think, that person is already mine. Mission accomplished. And that's where you fail. In a relationship, you are supposed to fall in love with the other person DAILY! It's about looking into their eyes and seeing the future with them. It's about communicating constantly with them. No fear. No holding back. You both saw something in each other at the start. And you both fell in love with each other. When you get into a relationship, one of the keys to longevity is trust. Trust them. Believe in them. Make goals together. Do things together. Build that foundation together. Love them. Adore them. Give them your heart. Give them your soul. They deserve it, and so do you.

Just close your eyes, allow me to take full control of all your thoughts. For tonight, I'll run my lips along your body.

(Inking my love all over your skin will be the way to create a whole new melody understood within the depth of your soul.)

Finding you was putting the final piece to my puzzled soul.

I got lost in the traces of my lips on your body.

Her body was a subject I couldn't fail. Tracing my lips on her skin was my way to study her. Blindfolding her was my way to touch her soul.

Allow me to be the victim of all your affections.

Just show me that unknown space between your heart and soul. Watch me unite them. Feel me pull all your feelings and emotions into one, and slowly see yourself glow in this world.

Never settle for that mediocre love. You deserve better. You deserve that pure rare love. The one that stirs up your soul.

It wasn't that love didn't exist. Love did exist. It was the communication that was lacking. That's a common problem nowadays in many relationships. We prefer to give our attention to our phones, instead of being in front of our partner. We prefer to go watch tv in the living room, instead of spending some time watching their favorite show with them. Drop the electronics for a day, and go spend time with your partner. Do not allow your heart and soul to get to the point of silence.

A WALK TO ETERNAL LOVE

Shower me with all your darkest thoughts, and watch my soul crawl into yours.

I may not be the one that you always dreamt of. I may not be the perfect person. I'm probably not the person that you see your future with. But, here is one rose. It's a special, one of a kind rose. It's a gift from the shadows of my soul. It resembles the love I have within. Perhaps my love is meant to be scattered around the world. But, this one rose is personalized just for you. Take care of it. Cherish it. Remember it.

Sink your heart into my soul, and watch us both drown in love.

Distance. It's the line that separated us, but it is the depth within us that keeps us together. If possible, I would twist the hands of time just to meet you in the past and bring you with me to the future. Just when I thought I could never love again, there you were, many miles away, just waiting patiently for my soul to find you. So close your eyes, feel my soul touch yours, and understand, that this is the powerful force of the unknown uniting our souls to mate for eternity.

Show me how much depth you have, and I'll gladly be there to see you spread your wings and fly.

It's not that she didn't know how to love. She was just worried about her future. She knew what she wanted, but she didn't know how to grab it. She knew the love existed, but didn't know if it was just her imagination or actually a reality.

A WALK TO ETERNAL LOVE

It was the depth of her eyes that made me believe in magic. She showed me how to enjoy life and leave all the pain behind. Never did I know I would find a whole, new world inside her soul. I grabbed her heart, accumulated all her thoughts, gave her a rose and said, "Forever you shall have my love in your soul." And if in doubt that my love truly exists, just close your eyes and remember, how beautiful it was to be touched and caressed by the eternal, powerful force of the unknown.

There is no measurement in this world to describe how much my soul can love you.

I put a little bit of love in her soul. My intention was to always bring out the emotions and feelings she had been holding inside. I saw daily how the colors of her eyes were coming back to life. I knew my time was coming to an end. But I had to give her all I had within. I had to make sure, that the love she had lost came back. And for that, I promised to forever protect her soul.

Don't try to understand what she is saying. Try to understand what she isn't saying. Just close your eyes and listen to her silence. It's one of the most beautiful ways to hear her soul.

I won't wish that you see yourself through my eyes. I'll make sure you feel how I feel when I see you through my eyes!

CARLOS MEDINA

I will search for you after death. And if the unknown decides to reincarnate you, I'll find you. I'll undress you from whatever you have become, and make pure love to your soul.

A WALK TO ETERNAL LOVE

It was in my dreams when I saw her the most. She floated by, leaving me with just the lingering taste of her heart. She knew exactly what to do to hypnotize all my emotions. It wasn't something she just figured out. She had studied me for a long time. She read all the scriptures describing the chaos and intensity I hold within. She didn't care how long ago they were written, for she felt an ancient soul like me didn't come around twice in a lifetime. The skepticism and worries haunted my mind just thinking: "How can she have so much power over my thoughts?" The conversation began by me describing how fucked up my past was. And without hesitation she said, "Just take my hand and bring me to your life and watch me show you that beautiful love you speak so much of."

What happens when we encounter a soul that is capable of playing and manipulating our emotions? We fall right into it. Why? We feel that for once we are loved, understood and cherished. And we fall into this deep hole that sometimes it's hard to get out of. It's normal. Humans go through this daily. Our action towards it, is what determines our destiny.

You may ask me, "how do we know when they are playing with our emotions?" Well, you'll see the signs. It's up to you to analyze and observe them. If they truly have feelings for you they would show you. They would at least try to match your love.

It's the way they speak to you. It has to be unique. If you see them speaking the same way to others, that's a big, red flag there. It's the way they act around you. Do they hide their phones? Do they take you around where they live? Have they allowed you to go to their home? Have they publicly said that they are in a relationship with you? Have they ever dedicated a song to you? Do they call you in the night or morning or middle of the night just to say, I wanted to hear your voice? Have they ever sent a random text message saying I miss you? Are you that person they think of during the day? Or just when they are bored.

All the signs are out there. It's up to you to see them. You will know if it's true love or just a pass time or just an ego stimulation. So, when you find that person who makes your whole soul gets rocked left to right, up and down. Analyze, observe. Make sure it's pure love. Not temporary shit. You're not here to fall for that new era romance bullshit. You want true, passionate love. And you deserve everlasting love.

And if one day you hear those sweet magical words come out. Understand that it comes from somewhere deep within. Hearing them will never be the same as feeling them. But if the day would come that you feel them, it's simply that I surrendered my mind, heart and soul to you.

When I love. It's never that typical love that you see all around. I make sure your whole world is turned upside down. When you begin to feel your heart pausing for a few seconds, it's me thinking of you. When you feel like screaming out loud for no reason, that's me, calling your name in the middle of the night. When you feel all your emotions and feelings being tampered with, that's just my way to show you the depth of the love I have within. And when you just can't help it and for some odd reason you feel this warmth within you. The one that your soul feels secured and safe... That's my way of saying, "I'm here for you. Heaven and hell can collide. And I'll be here for you. Not even Satan himself will interfere with the powers of the unknown."

Strap my words around your heart, and watch my soul make love to you.

Speak to me in a language that no one has heard and I'll assure you a response that's from the depth of my soul.

Just hold me in your arms like you did last night. The warmth of our bodies touching, two souls becoming one, two lovers syncing heartbeats.

Just put your hands in my soul and tell me, "I'm ready for you."

Tonight, I will run my hands through your soul. I shall touch every hidden corner that exists. It's my way of saying, "Thank You."

When we think about love, we think about magic, passion and romance. We create this fantasy in our minds of how it should be. We begin to visualize ourselves in this perfect world created from our precious thoughts. And it's alright. We are all dreamers. But guess what? To have that beautiful, romantic love that we all want so much, we must yank that dream to reality. We must make it our personal goal to live it and experience it. We can. It's possible.

But it all starts with you. You want a romantic person? Be romantic. You want someone passionate? Be passionate. You want someone with depth? Prepare yourself to have that depth. Pretty complicated shit that I'm talking about right? But in reality, it's not. Showcase your soul in every movement you make. Be honest. Love with integrity. Live with loyalty. Prepare your soul to build a strong foundation in a relationship.

If I surrendered and gave you my eternal love, would it be twisting the hands of fate? Or bending the hands of time by bringing the future to the present?

You stole my heart. Now let me build that bridge you always wanted.

What we have doesn't need to be defined. No regrets, just close your eyes and bring your soul to me. Let's let it go and allow it to be. Come closer, let me strip you so you can be worry free. Tonight, just do anything you want to me. I won't apologize for the way I'll make love to you. But I promise that tonight, I will ignite your soul and set it on fire.

I can't promise you that I'll be perfect. But I can promise you that I'll give you all the truth.

I can't promise you that it will be an easy ride. But I can promise you that I'll be there in the ups and downs.

I can't promise you the riches of this world. But I can promise you that I'll give you the most sacred treasure of all.

You'll have my heart beating next to you, every day. And if you feel that it's still not enough, remember, you'll have my soul for eternity and beyond.

Just put your fingerprints on my soul.
And watch me love you for eternity.

Hold me tight and never let go. If you believe in me and trust me, I can promise you love that's everlasting.

When in a relationship, couples have this thing of picking out nick names for their partners. Let's be realistic here. When you decide to pick a name for your partner, make sure it's something unique and special. Let's not hear - my queen/king or baby, sweet heart. Or whatever that new word is, `BAE'. Shine bright from the rest. After all, she/he is special to you.

If you had a chance to customize your soulmate.
What would you wish they had aside from love?

Awakened is my soul at the sound of your heartbeats.

(At your thoughts, I became reality.)

When I love. I give it my all. It's not, "Here, I'll give you this part of me and when you give me extra love, you'll get the rest." NO. I'm the type that will over flood your life with love. From the moment you wake up to the moment you fall asleep. And in the middle of the day, you'll get those random messages. The ones that will assure you that you are on my mind. That's just how I built myself. It was a must.

I love to go out. Although I prefer to stay home. But in order to keep the relationship alive, it's a must to dedicate some alone time and get out of the four walls. I'm the person that loves to showcase my love for my partner.

I love to go out with other couples and interact with them. Relationships nowadays need that. I'm that crazy guy that will wake up at 3am just to take a drive. No destination, just drive and drink coffee. I love to take one day and cook together as a couple should. It's a simple way to demonstrate that you are there for the other. I love baths. Especially with lavender scented candles all over. Let's not forget the wine.

When I love, it's not just to say I love this person and so on. I want to show it daily. I want the other person to know how I feel being with them. Not just knowing, I want them to feel my love for them.

Communication is a must with me. I love to talk and know if something is wrong or even if it's good. I may have a gift of being able to read others, but in a relationship I minimize that.

Why? Because I expect the other to openly tell me anything. Good or bad. For when two souls are in love and sharing a life as one, there shouldn't be anything to hold you back from speaking what you feel. But it is beautiful to finish each other's sentences.

A relationship could be the most beautiful thing you can have. Sometimes, it's us humans that fuck it up. So, let's love with all our heart and soul. And I can promise you, that your relationship will last longer than you think.

As my heart fell in to your hands, I became a prisoner to your soul. What you held deeply within is what kept me from leaving. No walls, no bars, no guards. Just your pure love caressing my soul and speaking many unspoken words.

Let's go hiking. Let's go biking. Grab your backpack and let's go camping. Fuck it! Let's just explore each other till eternity.

In a relationship, it's all or nothing. We need to make sure we give our entire soul to the other. We need to constantly demonstrate our love and affection. We cannot allow the fire to die. Cherish and adore each other. Keep the communication lines open at all times. Go back to the time of the courting stage. Remember the beauty you saw? Enchant them with the most powerful and charming words. Remember that time when you looked into their eyes? Do you remember what you felt? Look into their eyes again. Express to them what you hold within. Shower their soul with that love you hold so tight. Let it all out. And in return, grant them to be the exclusive holder of your soul.

We live a life telling ourselves that we will never find that person that would love us inside out. We go from relationship to relationship in hopes that they are the one. We sit here reading random poetry wishing that we were that writer's muse. We see couples walking in the streets holding hands or kissing, and our heart drops to the floor desiring that affection. We lay in our beds every single night just thinking about a person that we can't touch or have. We cry silently and put our hands together to pray to the almighty and request that he sends that soul soon to us. The one that will spend eternity with us.

Let's learn to love ourselves first. Let's send out love from within, exactly what we want in return.

You want depth? Give depth. You want that powerful soul love? Let's give powerful soul love. You want to attract a respectful, humble and honest person? Let's be that person first. You want someone to come and touch your soul? Begin to speak from your soul and watch the magic happen.

A WALK TO ETERNAL LOVE

It is important to remember that when taking your lady out, it is a time for both of you to spend together. Whether you take her to the beach, amusement park or just any place. It's a time for both of you to bond together. To cherish the company of each other. To communicate. To enjoy nature. To get out of the regular routine. Cherish the beautiful moments together.

Keyword- TOGETHER.

Relationships are all about commitments, sacrifices, elevations, unity, goals, communications, loyalty, trust, above all things mentioned, it's about that pure, deep love from the soul.

The moment will come when you will fall in love with someone. Make sure they are the right person. Speak to them with pure depth. Raise your standards. Listen closely to their unspoken words. Make sure you're included in their future plans. Keep the line of communication open at all times. It's the only way to really feel and understand them. Ask MANY questions. There is nothing wrong with that. But answer many questions too. Elevate the relationship to another level. Don't stay stuck in a phase. And if they are the shy one, go ahead and rip their soul out of their chest and watch the love they have hidden.

Fall in love with the person that wants to be by your side in the ups and downs of life. Fall in love with the person that will always be there for you in good and bad. Fall in love with the person that has goals. Fall in love with the person that is willing to sacrifice just to be with you. Fall in love with the person that will finish your sentence. Fall for that person that wants to rise in life by your side. Fall in love with that person that doesn't hide anything from you. Good or bad, their purity will be felt. Last but not least, fall in love with that person that will love you with all their soul.

Blindfolds on. Pillows on the floor. Bedsheets soaked in sweat. Room temperature rising. Bite marks on neck. Scratches on back. Mind stimulation. Soul penetration. Racing heartbeats. Two souls, reaching their destination.

Find the one that will be raw with you. And watch how beautiful their love will be.

Take their love and give it back to them ten times more.

Take my pain away. Show me the mask of an angel you wear. For tonight I will undress you, and dance with that devil within you. I'm not afraid, for I reside in the place between where many fear and most desire. That beautiful unknown.

It was hard to believe again, to feel again and to love again. But she knew life couldn't be lived without love. Her past was really painful but she promised herself, that she will do everything possible to make her future bright. She knew it was a sacrifice, but it was well worth it.

Take a good grip of my heart, for my soul is ready to elevate you.

Perhaps now we both could understand that two souls can sing and cry in harmony.

I love you. I can never deny how much love my heart feels for you. From the very first time I saw you, I couldn't resist the strong feelings for you. See, I saw your beauty within those beautiful eyes. I felt all that love you have underneath all those layers. Most importantly, I felt that pure soul of yours. I didn't care of your past, I just cared to be part of your present and for you to be a part of my future. Promise me one thing, please never change. Be you. Always be yourself. For I fell in love with all of you. And if one day, for some reason you begin to doubt in my love, remember me as the only person that loved every single corner of your soul and surrendered himself to you in whole.

When everything is going wrong, just place your head on my shoulder and listen to all the beautiful lullabies from my soul.

Allow me to be your personal architect. Let me grab all those shattered dreams and create a lifetime of love. Just close your mind and watch me reinvent all the desires from your soul.

There is no eternity if you are not by my side.

There is no forever if you are not sitting at its edge with me.

There will never be no depth in me if you don't feel my love within you.

After all these years, I still fall in love with you every day. Through all the bullshit, you stuck by my side. How could I not love you? You are my safety and security, forever you should have my soul. Perhaps my time is coming to an end in this world, but one thing you must know. I will find you in another lifetime, our souls will connect again my love, for we define the true meaning of soulmates. And I will fall in love with you all over again.

I studied you. Many centuries ago we crossed paths. I've been sculpting my soul for our next encounter. I promise you this time will be different. I won't drift away, I won't let go of you. This time, I`ll surrender it all just to spend eternity with you.

Can I be the one? Can I undress all the layers of you until I see your precious soul? Can I kiss all your scars and seal them with my love? Can I be the one to gather all the shattered pieces from your heart and place them exactly where you want? Can I be him? The one to forward the hands of time and show you how far we have come?

They said it was magic what we have. Two souls touching each other without physical contact. They questioned the integrity of our hearts, they just didn't know the purity was within our souls. We loved, we spoke, we laughed and made jokes to the sunrise. But the biggest illusion was merging two souls into one.

That's my problem. When I love, I don't sugar coat shit. When I say, I could touch your soul, that's because I know exactly how to. When I say, I could mend the pieces to your broken heart, that's because I already started the process. When I say, I will love you for eternity, that's because I know when I die, my love will live forever within your heart. And my soul will be felt in all the eyes you look at after my departure.

A WALK TO ETERNAL LOVE

I will search for you in every flower I see. I will look for you in every poem I read. I will recompose every syllable that crosses my mind in order to find you. For when the day comes that our eyes meet, we will leave all feelings behind and allow our souls to take full control.

There's this type of feeling you get when you cross paths with a rare soul for a second time. It's the same exact feeling you got the first time, just this time it's much stronger than before.

Sometimes we need to go through things prior to meeting again. Some of us evolve, some of us learn to understand and some of us go through more challenges to prepare our souls for the second encounter. When you finally meet up for the second time, everything picks up right where it was left off the first time. It's beautiful to reconnect and still see this person as a precious soul that's been sent from the unknown.

In my case, I evolved. I hadn't expected to feel your presence much deeper than before. I didn't think, that a second time around would bring up more emotions. I still believe that this universe brought our souls to meet. And it hurts me so much, that I can't be there by your side in the times you needed me the most. Or the times you just want to sit there and talk about the little things in life.

Have patience. I'm not really far away. When you feel weakness taking over, understand, my soul is there holding your hands. When doubt begins to cross your mind.. believe that I'm creating a foundation for generations to come.

At night while in bed, and you feel alone - trust me. TRUST ME. I'm there by your side. It may not be today. It may not be tomorrow. Sooner than later.. our spirits will meet. And we'll both understand, why this wait took so long.

I asked all the angels around me for advice. I didn't know what else to do or say. I didn't know what step I should take. For the first time in my life, I felt clueless. I drained myself emotionally and physically just to try and absorb a little of your pain. I was explained from a young age, that within me there is this power to take in all the negative and transform it into positive. And I tried. I really tried to take away all your pain. But somehow I felt like I lost that spiritual battle. Sometimes, I sit here and visualize all the different ways that I could help ease the pain. Even the way I could erase all your past and create beautiful memories that will last for eternities. I don't know how much more strength I have left, but I'm giving it all I have. And if you feel exactly what I feel... don't throw me back into the ocean. I'm not ready to be reincarnated just yet.

Here I am again. Letting it all go. Showcasing my soul to you. For the second time, we cross paths. Almost like the first time, yet stronger is this reconnection. I always meant every word I said. From the moment our souls spoke, to the moment that has yet to come. I know we have our share of a fucked up past. But I promise in due time, you won't have to face anything alone. I've been waiting for you for many centuries, and I could never stop until you knew, that I meant everything. I'll wait for you. I'll wait for you on top of that mountain. Where eternity meets infinity. Where you and I belong.

We cross paths daily with many people. One of them will be there for you. They will show you many beautiful things you have within. This individual is definitely a rare soul. As time goes by, you will learn something about this person. This individual will slowly help you open a portal to your soul. A gate you knew existed but didn't know exactly how to find it. You will cry. You will cry many times because this is a new you. This new you feels things differently. This you that you have found... this you... this you have evolved. Now you can finally say that you have found yourself within yourself. Now you're that rare soul.

If one day death decides to call me, I want you to remember me. Remember all the things that happened between us. Remember the endless hours we spent just talking about life. I also want you to remember every single word I said to you, every single promise and everything in between. You were the one that found that inner voice in me that no one ever heard. Slowly as time passed, you became part of my story. You became that beautiful silhouette in my memories. How could I not surrender my soul to you? It was a feeling, it was a must, because my promise has been to always be the protector of your fragile heart. Remember me. For it will be the only way, to find each other in the next life.

Promise me something. Promise me that ten or twenty years from now, you'll pull my book from your shelf and read it to your kids or grandkids. And when you read it to them... tell them. Tell them how I wrote about you and to you. And explain to them. Explain that the fairytales they wish and see on tv - Exists. If they believe. There is a such thing as deep pure love. Promise me that.

Maybe what you built with someone throughout the years is over. Now you look back and see all the damage that they did to you. You get all those negative thoughts that just keep drilling in your mind. Perhaps now, you feel like you're a ghost. You feel like you're walking this earth and no one sees you or feels your pain. You feel empty. You feel lonely. You feel abandoned. What happened, was meant to happen. What you went through, was meant to be walked by a person like you - a strong individual. All of it. All of that past... it's what brought you here today. It will help you build that strong foundation. Because now you know... you could never go back to that past. It's history. Take everything you learnt from it, and start rebuilding from within.

I hope one day you do find that person you've been looking for. I hope that this person shows you many beautiful things about you that you didn't know existed. I hope that they come in the exact moment when you really need them. I hope that this person comes and gives you a whole new understanding of what it is to be loved. I hope that this person cherishes you and stands by you in all the four seasons. Forever. These are my hopes for you. Because you deserve them. And you shouldn't settle for anything less.

I remember everything. I remember every single moment that we shared. Every single word, every feeling and every echo of your heart. From the first time we spoke to the moment when I shared all my feelings about you. I remember that night like it was yesterday. It was the first time in my life that I completely gave in to the power of love. I surrendered it all to you. My heart, my mind and my soul. All of it. I know how hard it is, to see things unfold that you never thought could become reality. To know that someone is willing to sacrifice a lot just for a taste of your pure love. It's amazing, isn't it? I will never regret anything that I said. I will continue to live by my words. My intentions were always to elevate things, to show you exactly what you deserve. Maybe this second time, is a verification, that I'm still me. No magic. No illusions. No fantasies. Just a human being, surrendering his soul. Showcasing what the human heart holds. I don't care what they think of me. At the end of the day, we all bleed and we all love.

Sometimes, I wonder, how can it be that I don't see you, but for some reason, I feel you in everything that I come across. Every breeze, every sunset, every dream, and every soul I come across. Each one shows me things that I never knew. I learn from them. I learn what not to do, and what must be done to give you a love, that millions seek. To give that love, that you so much deserve. Sometimes I close my eyes, and begin to imagine you by my side. No words being said. Just our souls finally resting in the presence of each other. A moment that we have been waiting for. A moment that's been written decades ago. A moment that's been seen many times by my soul. This journey is hard. Believing in things you don't see. Feeling things that you've never felt. Loving someone, because you actually know who they are inside. Knowing that what they have is exactly what you want. Putting your trust in that person. Placing your heart in their hands. I know. It's hard. I also know, that when it's true love... there is a connection that's formed. It starts from the very core of your soul. It never fades away. Because it's pure. It's delicate. It's rare. It's exactly a description of you. Of me. Of us.

A WALK TO ETERNAL LOVE

Tonight, I'll paint the sky with beautiful words. I will go where many have failed. I will let go of my human body to find you. I'll roam the dry deserts in search for you. I will let it all go just for a chance to touch you. Maybe now I have the strength to run. To run with no shadow following me, with no past attached to me. It's never hard to find you, because when I was blind, you lent me your eyes to see. Now how couldn't I be that replica of the love you seek? Forgive me, for I'm not there with you as we speak.

(I'm on my way to meet you, my seraph.)

Be the soul that transports pure love between galaxies and eternities.

A WALK TO ETERNAL LOVE

Love.
It's a unity of two souls. It's the beginning of a beautiful friendship that will turn into a precious family. It's giving your heart to someone that will cherish you and understand you. It's a feeling of security. It's like a dream that has finally happened. Being in love is like a river flowing within you and growing daily. To truly love someone, you must surrender it all, in order to live eternally in a relationship filled with magic and beauty. Never doubt in the powers of the unknown, what may seem like an illusion is actually someone else's reality.

I may not be with you physically but I am with you every step of the way. You may not see me, but believe me, I'm that presence you feel every day. At night, when you're twisting and turning, when your mind is going on full speed, I'm there silently whispering into your heart, "Everything, will be ok." When you feel the entire world on your shoulders, I'm there helping you understand that you're not alone. And when those tears decide to come out in full force, don't worry, I'm there kissing them away, hoping you can finally understand that my love is meant to secure you whole.

If I ever have the chance to meet you, remember that my soul is ready to surrender to you. I know exactly what kind of love you have within. I've been waiting for the moment when my reflection is right in front of me. When that moment comes, all sadness will vanish. No more lonely nights. I promise to be by your side, every step towards our eternity. I will never abandon you, I`ll forever carry your soul with my wings. Take my hand, let's create a path where none exists. Love is a powerful force that can guide our souls to a magical place.

I know one day, this search will be over. These
scattered pieces, will be collected and cherished
as one. This soul will sing in perfect harmony.
This spirit of mine, will kiss every part of you
that has been bruised. On that day, I will hold you
so tight that my love will overflow, and you'll feel
and understand, why it took so long for us to
meet. On that day, we will finally see through
each other's eyes. There will be no words to hide
in, and you'll see that all this time... I was
preparing the place that we shall call our home.

Maybe one day, I'll untie the ribbon around my heart for you. I won't be able to give you the moon or the stars as many people promise, but I'll give something that's worth more than all the galaxies combined. I'll give you a love that's been written in the souls of many, just so you know, this is what you brought out of me. Am I crazy for considering such a temple as you to surrender my soul to? Perhaps I am. This is just the way my love flows. You might wonder and ask the famous question, "why me? Out of all the people, why me?" And the answer is simple... I forever want to replicate that beautiful love we had in our prior life.

Tonight, I'll bring the beauty from my soul to you. I'll pour all my heart to you and show you how beautiful it feels to love someone from a place where only purity exists.

I never thought that I would cross paths with such beauty. After all, I have given my love to the wrong people many times. But I knew and felt, they were all guiding me towards you. They were all preparing me for that magical encounter.

It's amazing, this life we live in. We get hurt numerous times and at the end, there is actually a purpose for it all.

I had to go through it all. It was the only way for me to find myself. And when I thought I couldn't ever love again... I saw you. I saw so much pain in your eyes, so much worry, and so much love that was hidden for so long.

All of a sudden, I felt my old self again - the ability to tune in and to feel it all. I felt you. And I knew, we crossed paths a long time ago. I knew you were that adorable little girl, I gave those roses to. I knew it was you that took them with an open heart and cherished them. I could never forget, such a beautiful smile like the one you had that day.

May those roses be a symbol of the beauty I have within. May you understand, that our paths crossed because your soul has been requesting something unique and precious.

I'm here, surrendering it all, believing in what I don't see, and understanding, in what doesn't need to be understood.

To say that I love you, would be something similar to the others. But if I told you, close your eyes and feel me. I can assure you, it will be something that you never felt before. For what I see in you is something rare and unlike the rest. For that reason, I'll show you a glimpse of what it is to be loved by the depths of a pure soul. I'll strip all the thoughts from the pain that lingers. Give me the chance to pour everything I have hidden within me into your soul. I promise, you will feel an unconditional love. Because a soul like yours, deserves nothing less than purity.

I don't think I could ever stop loving the way I do. Because I've seen what true love is. I have felt it. Unlike anything else, it touched me deep inside my soul. For that, I could never stop. I could never stop demonstrating how precious you are. We have crossed paths before, and we departed just like the wind. But for some reason, we keep bumping into each other. For some reason, I find parts of you in every soul I come across, and each time, I see you, just like the very first time I laid eyes on your soul. How could I ever deny the existence of such a precious soul. How could I deny that I loved you, love you and will continue to love you for eternities, for infinities, beyond all the galaxies, from past to present, from now till death, from reincarnation to afterlife. I will love you.

I will go wherever you want me to go. But before we take this journey, walk with me. Come with me to this place that's deep inside of me. I promise you that you will never feel abandoned nor neglected.

ABOUT THE AUTHOR

Carlos Medina was born and raised in the Bronx, New York. He is known for sharing most of his talent on Instagram and Facebook. His writing began three years ago after a divorce from a five-year marriage. By sharing his past pain and healing, he began captivating his readers with his words as he has experienced different facets of life and has the ability to show you the vulnerability of your- self through his words. Traveling through the deepest crevices of your mind, exploring the passages of your heart, you'll be able to explore the depths of your soul and experience memories in ways you never did before.

CONNECT WITH THE AUTHOR

Carlos Medina

Website: magesoul.com
Email: magesoul@outlook.com
Instagram: magesoul
Facebook: magesoul
Twitter: magesoul

ALSO AVAILABLE BY THE AUTHOR

 WWW.MAGESOUL.COM

ALSO AVAILABLE BY THE AUTHOR

 WWW.MAGESOUL.COM

AVAILABLE

WWW.MAGESOUL.COM

JULY 2019

 WWW.MAGESOUL.COM

CHRISTMAS EVE 2019
LUMINOUS SOUL SERIES
By Carlos Medina

FOUR BOOKS

ONE PRICE

GREAT GIFT

   WWW.MAGESOUL.COM

AUTHORS:
Myke Duarte Carlos
Carlos Medina

AVAILABLE

   WWW.MAGESOUL.COM

AVAILABLE NOW

www.magesoul.com

Salted
Caramel Tears

by Natalie White

"The Soul speaks a language,
that words often fail to articulate.
I try anyway"

Come on a journey of healing
within Natalie's debut collection,
"Salted Caramel Tears"
as she carries you through
four chapters of Loss, Lessons, Love,
the final destination, Light.

COMING SUMMER 2019

www.magesoul.com

Magesoul Publishing is now accepting submissions from writers in the future who wish to get their book published through this corporation.

Submit or send inquiries to:
submissions@magesoulpublishing.com

www.ingramcontent.com/pod-product-compliance
Lightning Source LLC
Chambersburg PA
CBHW070614010526
44118CB00012B/1517